T0030412

Who Was
Duke Ellington?

by M. D. Payne

illustrated by Gregory Copeland

Penguin Workshop

We love you madly, Molly!—MDP

For Julianna and Ricky—GC

PENGUIN WORKSHOP
An Imprint of Penguin Random House LLC, New York

Copyright © 2020 by Penguin Random House LLC. All rights reserved. Published by Penguin Workshop, an imprint of Penguin Random House LLC, New York. PENGUIN and PENGUIN WORKSHOP are trademarks of Penguin Books Ltd. WHO HQ & Design is a registered trademark of Penguin Random House LLC. Printed in the USA.

Visit us online at www.penguinrandomhouse.com.

Library of Congress Control Number: 2020033624

ISBN 9780399539626 (paperback)   10 9 8 7 6 5 4 3 2
ISBN 9780399539633 (library binding) 10 9 8 7 6 5 4 3 2

Contents

Who Was Duke Ellington? 1

Edward Kennedy Ellington 5

A Life-Changing Sound 14

Here Comes the Duke! 26

From DC Sweet to NYC Gutbucket 36

Live from the Cotton Club 47

"It Don't Mean a Thing (If It Ain't Got That

Swing)". 58

"Take the 'A' Train" 76

"We Love You Madly" 84

"Retire to What?" 93

Beyond Category 100

Timelines 106

Bibliography 108

Who Was Duke Ellington?

In the summer of 1913, young Duke Ellington took a trip to Philadelphia that would change his life. He was heading to the City of Brotherly Love to hear the teenage piano master Harvey Brooks play. Duke had heard of Harvey's piano skills earlier that summer while vacationing in Asbury Park, New Jersey, and he was curious to see Harvey play live for himself. Harvey was fourteen years old at the time (the same age as Duke), and played a musical style that had swept the United States by storm—ragtime.

Duke had heard ragtime before. In fact, almost everyone in America had—ragtime was among the most popular musical styles in the country. But the way Harvey played the ragtime beat was different: Harvey's style was fast and flashy. His fingers bounced with a loose *oompah* rhythm. His hands ran across the piano keyboard with incredible speed, as if his fingers never touched the keys. And yet, the glorious melodies seemed to roll right off the piano. It was magic. Harvey had the entire crowd in the palm of his hand—including Duke.

When Duke got home to Washington, DC, all he wanted to do was play piano like Harvey. He practiced day and night on his family's piano. He searched clubs, pool halls, dance halls, cafés, and bars for ragtime piano masters who could play *like that*. In his search, he discovered a new world. He met and studied under musicians like Doc Perry, Lester Dishman, Claude Hopkins, Gertie Wells, Sticky Mac, and Blind Johnny, among others. He listened closely, and watched how they moved their arms when they played. Duke copied their style, even how they dressed. He asked them to show him how to make that unbelievable sound.

Duke watched and learned for years on end until he was such a good player that he wrote his own music—first just for piano, then for an entire jazz orchestra.

Once Duke started, he never stopped.

Duke, himself, became a piano master. Over a career spanning more than half a century, he wrote over three thousand songs, and told the story of African Americans in sound: protesting against the system that oppressed them and envisioning a future America filled with great hope and opportunity. Duke went on to become one of the greatest composers and musicians of the twentieth century—an artist truly beyond category.

CHAPTER 1
Edward Kennedy Ellington

Duke was born Edward Kennedy Ellington on April 29, 1899, to Daisy Kennedy Ellington and James Edward Ellington in Washington, DC—the capital of the United States of America.

James Edward (or "J. E.," as his family and friends called him) was a butler for a famous Washington doctor, and he occasionally catered parties at the White House.

Daisy was a stay-at-home mother who had given birth to one baby before Edward. That baby died soon after being born, so Daisy was extremely protective of Edward. She was always by his side.

Edward was a curious child with many interests. He spent most of his free time playing with his cousins, especially with his older cousin Sonny. Each Sunday, after Edward's mother took them to church, he and Sonny would visit all of their aunts and uncles that lived in the city of Washington. They'd eat cake and ice cream whenever someone offered it, which was most of the time!

Edward also liked to explore the great outdoors in and around his neighborhood with friends and cousins. They would climb trees in their backyards, walk all over the city, and play in the parks they discovered. But his biggest love was baseball. When Edward was a child, baseball was a new sport. His favorite team, the Washington Senators, started playing in the American League only two years after he was born.

Another new thing in Washington, DC, in the early 1900s was the automobile. But there weren't as many cars in Washington as in other American cities. Duke's hometown was modern in other ways—many homes

Washington
Senators jersey, 1901

already had electricity, and most major streets were lit with electric lights. Even so, horses were still what most people used when they didn't want to walk or use streetcars. One reason? The president of the United States, Theodore Roosevelt, preferred horses, and many people in the city wanted to be like him. Edward remembered seeing the president riding by on his horse as he and his friends played baseball.

When Edward was born, Washington had eighty-seven thousand Black residents—the largest number of any city in the U.S. Edward's family lived in the largest Black community in Washington and the entire United States at

the time: the U Street neighborhood. Edward's neighborhood was filled with Black music and art that couldn't be found anywhere else in the country. In fact, U Street was often called Black Broadway. The neighborhood was the center of Black culture and a symbol of stylish elegance in the city of Washington, even though the country had deep divides between Black and white cultures at the time.

Because Edward was Black, life was very different for him than for white children because of racial segregation.

Racial Segregation

After the abolishment of slavery in the United States, many white people still believed that Black people should not have all the rights and privileges that they did. Schools were all-Black or all-white. Some restaurants would serve only white people. There were separate entrances to buildings for Black and white people. Certain jobs were also white-only, meaning African Americans had limited work opportunities.

Keeping Blacks and whites separated was called racial segregation.

In 1954, the ruling of the Supreme Court in the *Brown v. Board of Education* case made segregation illegal in schools, and ten years later, the Civil Rights Act of 1964 outlawed racial segregation. The effects—unequal access to education, housing, and medical care—of this division, however, are still felt in the United States today.

Edward's family, friends, and a strong community protected him from the worst effects of segregation. The U Street neighborhood was filled with proud Black residents, strong Black businesses, and middle-class families just like Edward's.

Edward's father made enough money for his family to live well. Though they weren't rich, Edward said his dad "raised his family as though he were a millionaire." His father had a great sense of style and manners. He wore perfectly tailored three-piece suits. He could speak with anyone he

met with complete ease—something that Edward learned to do, too.

His mother did everything to make life comfortable and happy for him. Not only did she protect and spoil him, but she also instilled a sense of pride and hope in Edward. "You are blessed," she often told him—so Edward believed he could do anything.

CHAPTER 2
A Life-Changing Sound

During one of the many baseball games he played as a child, Edward was hit in the head with a baseball bat. His mother thought it was a good time for him to try something less dangerous. Edward started taking classical piano lessons. Both of his parents played piano very well. Edward often mentioned that his mother played so beautifully that it made him cry. She hoped that Edward would play piano, too, and forget all about baseball.

Edward attended the lessons, but he hated them. Everything was too stiff, too boring. Even his teacher's name was silly: Miss Clinkscales. He barely ever practiced, and he missed recitals. He wasn't interested in the music he was playing.

Baseball was still his favorite activity, and when Edward was in middle school, he figured out the perfect way to watch more baseball games. He got his first job selling peanuts at the

stadium where the Washington Senators played. But baseball wasn't the only sport he liked in middle school—he also started to play football and run track.

Edward was both athletic and stylish. He wore perfectly ironed button-down shirts with ties, crisp pants and suspenders, and polished shoes. His fashionable style and good manners got him his nickname. A friend called him "Duke," and it stuck.

As middle school ended, Duke had to choose his main subject of study in high school. His parents didn't think he had a future in sports, and Duke wasn't interested in music. But, he always loved to draw and paint, and his parents saw he had real talent. So, he chose to study art. Duke and his family knew he could make a good living creating art for posters, signs, flyers, magazines, and newspapers.

But just after Duke turned fourteen, he and his mother spent a summer at Asbury Park on the New Jersey shore. In a time before air conditioning, going to the beach was one sure way to escape the heat. While in New Jersey,

Duke worked as a dishwasher in the restaurant of a fancy hotel to earn a little extra spending money. He and the busboys talked all summer long to pass the time. They talked about sports.

They talked about girls. But most of all, they talked about the sound they heard coming out of the clubs and bars: ragtime.

In 1913, listening to a piano player live was the only way most people heard ragtime music. But Duke didn't hear any he really liked—that is, until the headwaiter at the restaurant where Duke worked told him that he should listen to Harvey Brooks play the piano. Duke sought him out, and was immediately inspired. "After hearing him," Duke said, "I said to myself, 'Man, you're just going to *have* to do it!'" He wanted to master the piano and play the way Harvey did.

When he returned that same year to Washington, DC, however, Duke started his art studies at the all-Black Armstrong Manual Training School. For the next few months, he would juggle art and sports at school, and his piano practice after school.

Ragtime

Ragtime is a type of piano music that was popular from the 1890s to the 1920s. It is known for the lively, bouncy rhythm that gives it a ragged feel.

It was first played by Black piano players in and around Saint Louis, Missouri, and soon spread throughout the country. Piano music was a big form of entertainment at the time. Many clubs and bars had piano players to attract customers, and people who owned pianos would buy sheet music to teach themselves popular ragtime songs at home. One of the most famous ragtime musicians was Scott Joplin, who was known for smash hits like "Maple Leaf Rag" (1899) and "The Entertainer" (1902). Ragtime was the first musical style created by Black Americans to quickly spread through all of American popular culture.

Duke also continued to work various jobs here and there, sometimes helping his dad with his catering business, sometimes working as a soda jerk (someone who served soft drinks and ice cream) at a soda fountain (a place where people came to drink sodas and eat sweets). The soda fountain also had a piano, which made the job even sweeter for Duke.

By this time, Duke just couldn't get enough of the piano. After school, he would go to pool halls and dance halls throughout Washington—places teenagers weren't supposed to be!—to learn from the piano masters.

He listened to and learned from dozens of piano masters, but he called Oliver "Doc" Perry his "piano parent." Doc would show Duke how to play tunes in his style, and he even taught Duke how to read music. Up until that point, Duke knew how to play music only from what he heard—a skill called playing by ear.

Doc had a very busy schedule, but he would always find time to teach Duke a few new things between his shows. Duke was an eager student—if the melody didn't sound right at first, he would practice over and over again until it did.

CHAPTER 3
Here Comes the Duke!

By his second year of high school, Duke was a decent piano player. So good, in fact, that he was asked to play at friends' parties. And people didn't just listen . . . they danced!

Duke enjoyed playing piano for fun, but he never thought it could be a career. Instead, he focused on his studies, and his future—becoming a commercial artist.

Still, the connections he had made with professional piano players led to some paid work. Duke was extremely outgoing, funny, and likable, and people wanted him to succeed. As he put it, "I have always seemed to encounter

the right people, the right places at the right time, and doing the right thing to give me the kind of instruction and guidance I needed."

Some of the more well-known piano players would let Duke play in their place when they were sick or just needed a day off. One day, while he was working at the soda fountain, the piano player was too sick to play. Duke jumped on the keys,

and made up a song on the spot—and it sounded great. That night, remembering what he played, he sat down at his own piano and wrote his first song, "Soda Fountain Rag."

Duke was becoming a composer—someone who can write music as well as play it.

When Duke was sixteen, his sister, Ruth, was born. Though his parents still gave him love and support, he was no longer the baby of the house.

Not that he needed support—Duke was ready to take on the world.

People asked him to play larger parties in the wealthier white communities of Washington, DC, and Virginia. Horse racing was a big form of entertainment in 1915, and Duke would play the parties that took place after the horse races.

Soon, he was so popular that people would skip the races and go to his parties instead.

Duke's piano playing improved throughout high school, and so did his artistic talent. In the fall of 1916, during his senior year of high school, he won a poster contest sponsored by the National Association for the Advancement of Colored People (NAACP). The prize was a college scholarship to Pratt Institute in New York City—one of the best places to study art in the country!

Duke had to make a tough decision. Would he accept the scholarship, give up music, and start a new life in New York City to focus on art full-time? Or would Duke jump into music feetfirst?

Music won. He dropped out of school a few months before graduating, in early 1917. At the young age of seventeen, he put together his own band with a few of his musical friends: the Miller Brothers (who played guitar, saxophone, and drums), twelve-year-old trumpeter Arthur Whetsel, and thirteen-year-old bassist and saxophonist Toby "Otto" Hardwick. They were known as The Duke's Serenaders, and they would play music for special occasions in and around Washington. Not to mention, they began to play a new sound that grew and developed from ragtime—jazz.

Jazz had a rhythm similar to ragtime, but it was smoother and much less bouncy. Jazz songs often don't have many lyrics—in fact, the melody is the driving force behind the song. Jazz is based on a feeling. It's a pulse that is created by the musicians. Performers play long solos—moments of the song during which they play whatever inspires them while still matching the overall mood of the music. This is known as improvisation.

The Duke's Serenaders played this new jazz sound "sweet" as Duke would put it. Everyone played their instruments softly, oftentimes as background music for fancy parties. He always made sure his band sounded—and looked—as stylish as possible for his fashionable audience. He also knew how to make an entrance. Whenever he was about to perform at a club or dance hall, he would have a friend open the door and announce: "Get out of the way, 'cause here comes the Duke!"

Duke and his band hit their stride just as the world began to change around them. On April 6, 1917, America joined a war that had been raging in Europe since 1914: World War I (WWI). Germany had already taken over most of Europe, and was going to invade France and Britain. Americans had anxiously watched events in Europe for three years, but it was clear that France and Britain needed more support to push back against the Germans.

British soldiers in the trenches during World War I

Duke didn't join the war effort as a soldier, but he helped in other ways. He stayed in Washington and worked as a messenger for the State Department and was later moved to the navy's transportation division.

During WWI, Washington was the center of the American war effort. There were many new visitors to the nation's capital—military officers and foreign diplomats—who didn't know which bands to hire for their parties and events. So, Duke put ads in local newspapers and phone directories as if his band

were the most popular dance band in Washington, DC. The calls came pouring in! In fact, he got such a big response that he began to manage other bands to make sure he could respond to every request.

Both WWI and Duke's job at the State Department ended in November 1918. Duke was then getting a lot of gigs by playing with his band and managing other people's as well. But he still needed another job to make ends meet. So, he made use of his artistic skills and opened up a sign-making business. This new work fit perfectly into his dance band work. He'd make signs for the parties he was playing. When someone asked him to make a sign for their party, he'd ask if they had a band yet. It was a good way to get both jobs.

Duke had a busy schedule of music and sign making. But he became a family man as well. He married Edna Thompson on July 2, 1918, and their first and only child, Mercer Kennedy Ellington, was born on March 11, 1919.

CHAPTER 4
From DC Sweet to NYC Gutbucket

For four years, Duke worked hard at his music and sign making, and he soon had the best jazz band in Washington, DC. As players left the

Serenaders, Duke replaced them with even better ones. Although the demand for his music—and the growing demands on him as a father—were high, Duke set his sights elsewhere. He wanted to get to New York City.

New York City, 1920s

Wilbur Sweatman

In March of 1923, Duke's luck changed. Wilbur Sweatman, a popular New York City musician, asked Duke's new drummer, Sonny Greer, to come and play in his band. Sonny agreed—but only if Duke and Otto could come along. So, Duke packed his bags and headed for New York. He left Edna and their four-year-old son, Mercer, behind, until he could earn enough money for them to follow.

New York City was completely different from Washington, DC. Cars zoomed along the avenues, and streetcars clattered above and below the busy streets. Tall buildings loomed over Duke during the day, and at night, the city glowed. New York City never slept—there was always something going on somewhere, no matter how late. Duke,

Sonny, and Otto arrived in Harlem, in Manhattan. In 1923, the neighborhood was buzzing with a new creative spirit, and Duke, yet again, found himself just at the right place and time— the Harlem Renaissance.

The Harlem Renaissance

The Harlem Renaissance of the early twentieth century was an exciting movement of Black writers, musicians, dancers, artists, and thinkers who were inspired by the bustle of city life and the music of the South. The streets came alive with the bold new sound of jazz, and the neighborhood flourished with art by painters like Charles Alston,

Charles Alston

music by performers like Louis Armstrong, and stories by writers like Zora Neale Hurston. People read fiction and poetry by Black authors along with books about race and the role of Black culture in America.

Zora Neale Hurston

The constant exchange of new, exciting ideas helped Black people create a community rooted in their own culture. These new ideas spread not just all over New York City but throughout the United States as well.

Every street in Harlem was a new adventure for Duke, Sonny, and Otto as they experienced Black music and culture from all over the world. But with all this competition, it was hard for them to stand out. And when Duke, Sonny, and Otto left Wilbur's band, they just couldn't find work on their own. Within weeks they ran out of money for food. They had no choice but to pack up and head home to Washington.

But Duke didn't give up. He returned to New York City with his band just a few weeks later. And his persistence paid off. He played for a famous singer, Ada Smith, and she asked the band to perform with her. They played the Exclusive Club, which was a perfect fit for the sophisticated "sweet" music that they had played in Washington.

Ada Smith

By the summer of 1923, Duke had made enough money to send for Edna and Mercer. The family moved into an apartment of their own in Harlem. The band had moved on from Ada Smith, and was then known as The Washingtonians. They played night after night, and Duke built up his talent and reputation.

Duke and The Washingtonians

He also began to write and sell songs for extra money. The songs were published as sheet music, which could be sold all over the country. But none of the songs felt quite right. Duke still wasn't writing and playing the kind of music that most people were coming to Harlem to hear: a grittier sound called gutbucket, that had come from New Orleans, in the South.

Saxophone, trumpet, and trombone players from New Orleans who came to New York City would make their horns growl or make *wah-wah* sounds (waving the rubber part of a toilet plunger over their horn!) so their instruments sounded like human voices. Duke was inspired by the new sound, but he didn't know how to play it himself. Only when Duke added trumpeter Bubber Miley to The Washingtonians in September 1923 did everything change. Bubber could make his horn growl and wah-wah—and it completely shifted the band's sound. "He used to growl all night long, playing gutbucket on his horn. That's when we decided to forget all about the sweet music," Ellington recalled of Bubber's playing.

Bubber Miley

Shortly after adding Bubber to the band, Duke signed a long-term contract with the Kentucky Club, a jazz club in Manhattan's Midtown neighborhood. The band became known as Duke Ellington and His Kentucky Club Orchestra. It expanded to ten people, barely able to fit on the small stage—but they made an amazingly big, amazingly unique sound. Duke took other people's songs, like W. C. Handy's "St. Louis Blues," and put a new spin on them. He added strange sounds, like the deep rumble of the saxophone to mix the gritty in with the sweet.

Duke Ellington and His Kentucky Club Orchestra worked tirelessly to sharpen their skills, playing night after night until the sun rose. And people were starting to notice.

CHAPTER 5
Live from the Cotton Club

By 1926, jazz music had become the most popular music in America, and Duke Ellington and His Kentucky Club Orchestra were the hottest jazz band in New York City. People packed into the tiny nightclub to hear them. Up on the bandstand, Duke and his band, dressed in tuxedos, put on an amazing show.

Everyone had a great time—especially Duke, who played his piano with a smooth style and

Irving Mills

easy smile.

One night, a music publisher, Irving Mills, heard Duke and the band play "Black and Tan Fantasy," a new song that was a perfect example of Duke's one-of-a-kind sound, and Irving instantly knew that he had found something special.

Irving introduced himself to Duke after the show, and asked if he could be the band's manager. He had two big ideas for how to get Duke's sound out of the tiny Kentucky Club and to the rest of America: First, he thought they needed to make records of Duke's songs. At the time, most Americans had a record player in

their home, and would buy and play records—
flat-plastic recordings—of their favorite artists'
songs. Second, Irving wanted them to play in a
bigger club. And in December of 1927, he had
the perfect place in mind: the Cotton Club, one
of the top music spots in New York City—and
the country—during the Roaring Twenties.

The Roaring Twenties

Everything about life in the 1920s—nicknamed "the Roaring Twenties"—seemed to be moving quickly. Women got the right to vote in 1920, fast cars were on roads everywhere, airplanes were a common sight in the sky, and skyscrapers climbed higher and higher. America was at peace after the end of World War I, and business was booming. People were leaving rural life for the buzz of big cities like New York and Chicago. In urban restaurants and clubs, fashionable women known as flappers wore headbands with feathers, and shiny necklaces. Men were dressed in crisp three-piece suits, sometimes wearing top hats and coattails. People danced to the sound of hot jazz—which became the soundtrack for the 1920s, which had another nickname: "the Jazz Age."

To play at the Cotton Club, Duke needed an even bigger band. Along with Duke, there were now eleven musicians on a much larger stage! Sonny Greer was perched above the orchestra with a massive drum kit that expanded out into bells, gongs, and all kinds of other percussion

instruments. And the musicians weren't alone onstage. There were dancers, comedians, and other entertainers. People would come for dinner, and stay for the music and entertainment that began at 9:00 p.m. The party didn't end until the next morning. Duke was at the center of it all.

But there was one big issue: the Cotton Club was a segregated venue, and—even though the entertainers were Black—only white people were allowed to watch the show. The stage was also sometimes decorated to look like a southern plantation in the time of slavery, complete with slave cabins painted in the background. The Cotton Club's owner, Owen "Owney" Madden,

Owney Madden

wanted to profit off of this new creative hot spot that seemed to bring in a lot of customers. But he saw Black people only as the entertainment or the help—even in their own neighborhood.

Duke forged onward at the Cotton Club, growing as a songwriter and becoming more popular. A pianist of many styles, he learned to write music for any occasion, for every feeling. And even though most of the residents of Harlem couldn't see his show live, Duke's music became a staple of the Harlem Renaissance through his recordings.

Mildred Dixon

At home, there were big changes for Duke. In early 1929, Duke separated from Edna, and they never lived together again. Duke's new partner, Mildred Dixon, helped Duke raise Mercer.

These big changes at home occurred just as Duke's career began to skyrocket. In fact, Duke got his biggest break so far in 1929 when the music he played at the Cotton Club was broadcast live on CBS radio to the whole country. Most people then had a radio in their homes and, throughout America, everyone tuned in to listen to—and dance to!—the music of Duke Ellington. Movies were another great way for Duke and his music to be noticed by new audiences, and that same year, he appeared in *Black and Tan,* an important short film about the struggles and achievements of African American artists during the Harlem Renaissance.

Duke was just getting started.

CHAPTER 6
"It Don't Mean a Thing
(If It Ain't Got That Swing)"

In 1929, Duke Ellington was on the top of the Harlem music scene. His music was heard everywhere on the radio. He dipped his toes into the film business. He had more money than his parents had ever earned.

He asked his mother, father, and sister Ruth to move north and join him, Mildred, and ten-year-old Mercer in New York City. But just as Duke reached the top of his fame, the American stock market crashed. The Roaring Twenties ended, and the Great Depression began.

New York Stock Exchange building after market crash, 1929

The Great Depression

The Great Depression started on October 29, 1929, when the American stock market crashed, and with it, much of the US economy. Twenty thousand companies went out of business. More than sixteen hundred banks were forced to close,

which caused American citizens to lose their homes, their businesses, and their life savings. The situation grew worse when, just four years later, in 1933, it was estimated that one in every four Americans was out of work.

Lasting for a decade, the Great Depression was one of the worst financial disasters in modern history.

Duke worried that the Great Depression would affect his band's ability to earn a living. But through the rest of 1929 and 1930, he and his band continued to wow audiences at the Cotton Club, on the radio, and on tour. He wrote more music and appeared in more movies.

Despite all the changes in the country and at home, he still recorded nonstop, making about 160 records between 1927 and 1931. In 1931, when many Americans hit an all-time low, Duke had his first big nationwide hit with "Mood Indigo." It was also around this time that Duke made plans to leave the Cotton Club. Duke and the Cotton Club Orchestra had played there for four years. But he yearned to write songs that were truly "the music of my people," and spend more time touring with his band.

While in Chicago, Duke met a singer named Ivie Anderson, and he was so impressed by her, he asked her to be in the band. In 1932, he recorded his now legendary song, "It Don't Mean a Thing (If It Ain't Got That Swing)" with

Ivie Anderson

Ivie singing vocals by Irving Mills. "It makes no diff'rence if it's sweet or hot / Just give that rhythm ev'rything you've got / Oh, it don't mean a thing, if it ain't got that swing" she sang over the bold roar of the trumpets and the deep hum of the bass. What was "swing"? It was a new style of upbeat jazz music that made people want to *swing*—as in dance—their blues away. Duke had helped invent this new lively sound. Soon, it would be the next musical craze, with bands playing swing music throughout the country.

The popularity of songs like "Mood Indigo" and "It Don't Mean a Thing (If It Ain't Got That Swing)" allowed Duke to tour Europe. Starting in June 1933, Duke and the band played in the United Kingdom, the Netherlands, and France. His tour was a huge success. He even met with royalty in the United Kingdom.

The Prince of Wales asked to play the drums with the band at a private party one night, which Duke happily allowed. By the end of the night, the two men acted like old friends—Duke called the Prince "The Wale" while the Prince gave Duke the nickname "The Duke of Hot."

Duke meeting the royal family of the United Kingdom

Duke Ellington and His Orchestra returned to the United States in August 1933 and continued to tour, but during the time of segregation, not every white person wanted a Black band playing in their neighborhood—especially in the American South. It was in the South that Jim Crow laws were most strongly enforced.

In areas with harsher Jim Crow laws, Duke and his orchestra toured in two private train

cars, known as Pullman cars. The Pullman cars were luxurious, large, and they had everything he and the band needed—including beds. Duke Ellington and His Orchestra had a safe place to rest after a long night's work. With the Pullman cars, Duke was able to play many more dance halls and reach a larger audience while on tour in the United States.

Jim Crow Laws

After the Thirteenth Amendment to the US Constitution was signed into law in December 1865, states in the American South quickly created laws that guaranteed that former slaves would remain "separate." These laws were called Jim Crow laws. They made it illegal for Black people

to go into many restaurants, stores, and other businesses. Black people could not ride in the front section of a bus or even sit anywhere but in the balcony of a movie theater. Whites Only signs became common. And if Black people even tried to bend the rules, they could be thrown in jail.

Jim Crow laws were made illegal by the Civil Rights Act of 1964.

Still, Duke wanted to do more than tour. He decided to take everything he had learned as a composer and write longer pieces that truly reflected the Black American experience.

As a result, in 1935, Duke starred in the movie *Symphony in Black: A Rhapsody of Negro Life* alongside jazz singer Billie Holiday. The musical short

film centered on a performance of Duke's nine-minute composition "A Rhapsody of Negro

Billie Holiday

Life." The piece was split into four parts, each representing a particular part of Black life—from blue-collar workers to love and heartbreak to spirituality to nightclub dancing. With this music,

Scene from *Symphony in Black*

Duke was able to not just entertain, but compose
a work that revealed a life of hardship and joy
experienced by most Black people.

These stories were rarely, if ever, taught in school, and with "A Rhapsody of Negro Life," Duke was able to show the humanity of Black Americans. The movie received high praise and later went on to win an Oscar—the highest achievement in the movie industry.

The fun didn't stop there: Duke Ellington toured nonstop through the late 1930s.

In 1939, he and his band went back to Europe for three months. When they arrived in France, the French people greeted Duke like a hero. When he celebrated his fortieth birthday in Stockholm, Sweden, fans packed his dressing room with flowers!

German soldiers marching during the start of World War II, 1939

But not every place was so wonderful in Europe. The band wasn't allowed to play in Germany, where jazz was banned and World War II, one of the deadliest wars in human history, slowly but surely began to take shape.

CHAPTER 7
"Take the 'A' Train"

Duke didn't waste much time after returning from his second European tour. He immediately formed Tempo Music, a company to manage his compositions. The company would collect royalties—money owed to him any time someone played one of his songs. He asked his little sister,

Ruth, to take charge and run the company so that he could focus on touring and writing new music.

Duke also had someone to help him write new music: Billy Strayhorn.

Duke Ellington and Billy Strayhorn

Billy Strayhorn (1915–1967)

Billy Strayhorn was born in Dayton, Ohio, but spent many months of his childhood with his grandparents in North Carolina. He seemed to love his grandmother's piano from the moment he could reach up and  play it. Billy attended the Pittsburgh Musical Institute for a time, and became a classically trained music composer and arranger. He wrote several songs that became jazz classics—including "Lush Life" and "Take the 'A' Train." He worked with Duke Ellington as his musical partner for nearly thirty years.

Billy met Duke in 1938. And he could play Duke's songs in a way that really impressed Duke. Instantly, Duke asked Billy to work on writing new arrangements for some of his songs. When Billy was supposed to meet him in New York, Duke told Billy he could take the A train (part of the New York City subway) to get to Harlem.

When Billy arrived, he had the new arrangements. Inspired by the bouncy excitement of the New York City subway, Billy had also written a brand-new song for Duke called "Take the 'A' Train."

"Take the 'A' Train" was recorded in 1941 and soon became a hit. In fact, Duke opened every single concert with that song. After that, Duke and Billy became an unstoppable writing duo, going on to create hits like "Ko-Ko," "Cottontail," and "In a Mellow Tone." Duke was more popular than ever before.

With the help of Billy, Duke was writing even more music—at home, on tour, everywhere! Duke wrote music inspired by the musicians he played with, so he never finished a tune until he was playing it with the band.

This took quite a bit of time, and he'd often write music up until the last minute Duke and his orchestra were due onstage! As Duke said, "I don't need time. What I need is a deadline."

Duke's success came just as the violence of World War II reached the United States. When the Japanese attacked Pearl Harbor on December 7, 1941, America declared war on Japan and its allies, the Axis Powers, which included Germany and Italy. Millions of

Americans rushed to the fight across the Atlantic and the Pacific. Duke's son, Mercer, who had studied composition and even written a few songs for his father, joined the army.

Pearl Harbor attack, 1941

Duke supported the war effort by appearing on radio and film to ask Americans to buy war bonds—investments in the war. American

War bond

soldiers, fighting in countries all over the world, listened to swing radio and records, including Duke's music, and thought of home.

During the war, Duke worked hard to write an even longer piece of music—his first-ever jazz symphony at Carnegie Hall.

With *Black, Brown and Beige* in 1943, Duke spoke out against racial injustice. But his powerful music was also filled with hope and positivity—a celebration of Black American culture. In an era of segregation, as more people took to the streets to protest the mistreatment of Black

Americans, Duke used his music as his own form of resistance.

Duke could at last be counted among the greatest American composers of the twentieth century. But, when the war ended in 1945, so did the swing craze—and Duke's popularity. Rock 'n' roll was on the rise, and soon Americans would be dancing to a new beat.

CHAPTER 8
"We Love You Madly"

Bill Haley and His Comets

In the early 1950s, Duke's band was one of the few swing bands still popular enough to continue to tour. In 1954, the song "Rock Around the Clock" by Bill Haley and His Comets was the most popular song in America.

It seemed that even Duke couldn't compete with rock 'n' roll. Duke and his orchestra still played shows throughout America. Duke's son, Mercer, played with the band, sometimes on trumpet and sometimes on saxophone. The audiences were smaller, but Duke was always grateful for his audiences, telling them at the end of every show, "We love you madly."

The tides began to turn, however, in 1956, when Duke was asked to perform at the Newport Jazz Festival.

The Newport Jazz Festival

Newport, Rhode Island, was worlds away from the tiny, dark jazz clubs of New York City. In July 1954, however, it was the site of the first Newport Jazz Festival. Fans from Boston, New York, and around the country gathered outdoors for three

days to listen to the very best jazz performers, including Ella Fitzgerald and Billie Holiday.

The festival remains so popular that it is still a yearly event, featuring the biggest names in jazz. The Newport Jazz Festival also raises money to provide instruments and music education to children around the United States.

The band performed one of the first long pieces Duke had ever written—"Diminuendo and Crescendo in Blue." The band roared to life on the stage, and the saxophonist, Paul Gonsalves, played a jazzy, explosive solo for more than six minutes. When the song ended, Duke couldn't even speak over the cheers to tell the audience he loved them madly right back.

Duke's music was a hit once again! Columbia records, one of the biggest jazz record labels in the country, released an album of the stunning performance, which became Duke Ellington's best-selling album.

Duke, who was then fifty-seven years old, still had the energy of a teenager. In addition to his normal output of short jazz songs, he took on new and interesting projects. With Billy, he created music inspired by the plays of William Shakespeare and wrote music for major Hollywood films. In 1960, Duke and

Billy also created a jazz version of the famous Christmas-themed ballet, *The Nutcracker Suite.*

Duke had to learn how to say "We love you madly" in dozens of languages for tours around the world. In 1963, he traveled to India, Iran, Iraq, Jordan, Lebanon, Pakistan, and Sri Lanka. In 1964, he went to Japan. Duke and Billy Strayhorn wrote new compositions based on their travels, including *Far East Suite.* In music, a *suite* (say: sweet) is a series or sequence of short songs. From 1964 into 1965, Duke also wrote his most spiritual work to date—*First Sacred Concert*. He worked with popular gospel singers and performed the concert in churches around the country. The *Far East Suite* and *First Sacred Concert* turned out to be some of his best work. *Far East Suite* won a Grammy Award and was named Record of the Year by jazz music magazine *Downbeat*.

When asked what his favorite piece of music was, Duke would often say it was his next—the one he hadn't even written yet. Mercer Ellington became the band's manager in 1965 so that Duke could focus on writing new songs. That meant someone Duke completely trusted would be in charge of the business.

Duke and Mercer Ellington

Shortly afterward, Duke went to Dakar, Senegal, in Western Africa to play at the first-ever World Festival of Negro Arts in April 1966, a life-changing experience for the musician.

At the height of his newfound fame and creativity, however, the unimaginable happened—Billy Strayhorn died of cancer on May 31, 1967. At Billy's funeral, Duke, a man who rarely showed emotion, gave a stirring speech. "Billy Strayhorn was my right arm [and] my left arm." Duke said.

When asked if he was going to be all right, Duke said, "No, I'm not going to be all right!" Many wondered if Duke would be able to continue.

CHAPTER 9
"Retire to What?"

Despite Billy's death, Duke continued to tour and write new music. In 1968, his *Second Sacred Concert* was performed. He created so much music, some pieces were played only once—they were never recorded or written down. Although he never graduated from college, he traveled around the country to receive honorary music degrees from many colleges and universities. At each college and university, he played new music, written in honor of the occasion.

Duke had more to celebrate than his seventieth birthday on April 29, 1969. On that day, President Richard M. Nixon presented him with the Presidential Medal of Freedom.

The president also played "Happy Birthday" on the piano just for Duke. In his speech, Nixon said, "In the royalty of American music, no man swings more or stands higher than the Duke."

The Presidential Medal of Freedom

President John F. Kennedy chose the Americans who would be awarded the Presidential Medals of Freedom. Author E. B. White, singer Marian Anderson, and artist Andrew Wyeth were among the first recipients in 1963. Along with the Congressional Gold Medal, the Medal of Freedom is the highest honor that can be given to someone who is not in the US military. Only a few individuals are awarded the Presidential Medal of Freedom each year. Many fields are recognized, including art, science, medicine, and education.

Other entertainers who have received the award include Walt Disney, Steven Spielberg, Oprah Winfrey, Stevie Wonder, and Rita Moreno.

Life on the road fueled Duke. While other performers may have had visions of heading to a quiet life away from the stage, Duke continued to travel around the world and compose wherever he could: backstage, in hotel rooms, and on trains, planes, and in cars. Whenever someone asked him if he was ready to retire, he'd respond, "Retire to what?"

In 1971, Duke released *New Orleans Suite*—a celebration of the music and musicians of New Orleans, who had influenced him. Duke was still creating music with a fresh point of view and inspiring young jazz musicians around him.

Duke continued to tour nonstop. He traveled to Asia in 1972, at the age of seventy-three. Shortly upon his return home, he got the frightening news that he had lung cancer. But even that didn't convince him to retire. He finished writing *Music Is My Mistress,* the story (in book form) of his life. He finished his *Third Sacred Concert.* And then he left in 1973 on another world tour, traveling throughout Africa and then Europe.

Also in 1973, Duke even appeared in his own television special called *Duke Ellington . . . We Love You Madly!* On the show, which featured stars such as Aretha Franklin and Ray Charles, Duke played with his biggest jazz band to date: fifty-three musicians!

Ray Charles and Aretha Franklin

In 1974, when he had grown too sick to leave the hospital, Duke kept a keyboard by his side so that he could continue working on new music. And he kept right on working. Duke Ellington died in New York City on May 24, 1974, three weeks after his seventy-fifth birthday, with his family by his side.

But his legacy lives on.

CHAPTER 10
Beyond Category

Mercer Ellington and the Duke Ellington Orchestra

After Duke's death, Mercer took over as leader of the Duke Ellington Orchestra. The band continued to tour around the world and share Duke's music with a growing audience.

Shortly after Duke's death, the Duke Ellington School of the Arts was founded in Washington, DC, not far from where Duke was born. It trains students to pursue their dreams, work through hardships, and meet other aspiring, determined musicians. Just like Duke did.

Duke's music is studied at colleges and universities around the country. High-school jazz bands continue to play Duke's music. In fact, every year, the best high-school jazz bands from throughout the United States travel to New York City to celebrate Duke's music and compete in Essentially Ellington.

Essentially Ellington

Jazz at Lincoln Center is an organization dedicated to supporting and celebrating jazz. Each year, it holds the Essentially Ellington competition. The Jazz at Lincoln Center organization selects Duke Ellington compositions and distributes them with sheet music to high schools throughout the United States. Jazz bands at these schools then send a recording of their performance back to be judged. The best musicians and performers are invited to New York City to take part in musical workshops dedicated to Duke Ellington and compete onstage.

Duke Ellington showed the world what a jazz musician could be. He influenced more jazz players than any other musician of his time. And, as a composer, he created thousands of songs for future generations, forever changing the sound of jazz.

He won eleven Grammys, including for lifetime achievement in 1966. In 1999, there were celebrations around the world in honor of the hundredth anniversary of his birth.

In 2001, he appeared on the Washington, DC, edition of the US quarter—the first Black American to appear on US currency.

Duke was known as the King of Jazz in Europe, and as having the finest swing band in America. But he disliked being put into categories—he said that the best kind of music is "beyond category."

Duke wrote music that celebrated the beauty of Black Americans, like "Black and Tan Fantasy." He wrote about the exciting energy of Harlem and its thriving Black community with songs such as "Harlem River Quiver." The growls of his musicians highlighted the struggles of Black Americans—and the joys. Duke used his music to protest the segregation and racism he had witnessed since he was born. During the American civil rights movement, "Come Sunday," a song from *Black, Brown and Beige*, became an anthem sung at marches.

Later in life, Duke said that he wrote music not only "of my people" but "of *the* people." The world had changed greatly from when Duke was a boy in Washington, DC, to when he played his last concert—and he changed along with it. But all the while, the world loved Duke madly.

Timeline of Duke Ellington's Life

1899 — Born Edward Kennedy Ellington on April 29 in Washington, DC

1915 — Writes his first song, "Soda Fountain Rag"

1917 — Starts his first band, The Duke's Serenaders

1918 — Marries Edna Thompson

1919 — Son, Mercer, is born

1923 — Moves to Harlem, New York City

1927 — Begins a four-year engagement at the Cotton Club

1929 — Separates from Edna Thompson

— Nationwide weekly broadcast debuts on CBS Radio

— Stars in his first film, *Black and Tan*

1931 — Has first hit record, "Mood Indigo"

1933 — Tours Europe for the first time

1938 — Meets Billy Strayhorn

1943 — *Black, Brown and Beige* premieres at Carnegie Hall

1956 — Appears at the Newport Jazz Festival

1965 — Performs the *First Sacred Concert* in San Francisco

1966 — Receives a Lifetime Achievement Grammy Award

1969 — Awarded a Presidential Medal of Freedom

1971 — Releases *New Orleans Suite*

1974 — Dies on May 24 in New York City

Timeline of the World

1899 — Sheet music of "Maple Leaf Rag" by Scott Joplin sells over 100,000 copies its first year

1908 — Ford Motor Company produces the first Model T car on its assembly lines

1917 — United States enters World War I

— The Original Dixieland Jazz Band records the first jazz record, "Livery Stable Blues"

1918 — World War I ends

1919 — Chicago race riots spark protests in twenty-nine cities around the United States

1927 — Charles Lindbergh completes the first solo transatlantic flight

1929 — American stock market crashes; the Great Depression begins

1941 — United States enters World War II

1945 — World War II ends

1955 — Modern civil rights movement begins in Montgomery, Alabama

1957 — The Soviet Union launches Sputnik I, the first artificial earth satellite, into space

1964 — The US Civil Rights Act is passed

1974 — President Nixon resigns due to the Watergate scandal

Bibliography

*Books for young readers

Chilton, John. *Who's Who of Jazz.* New York: Da Capo Press, 1985.

*Crease, Stephanie Stein. *Duke Ellington: His Life in Jazz.* Chicago: Chicago Review Press, 2009.

Ellington, Edward Kennedy. *Music Is My Mistress.* New York: Da Capo Press, 1973.

*Pinkney, Andrea Davis. *Duke Ellington: The Piano Prince and His Orchestra.* Illustrated by Brian Pinkney. New York: Jump at the Sun, 1998.

Shadwick, Keith. *The Encyclopedia of Jazz and Blues.* London: Quintet Publishing Limited, 2001.

*Venezia, Mike. *Duke Ellington.* New York: Children's Press, 2018.